IN THIS SERIES

THE COMPOSITE GUIDE

to STRONGMAN COMPETITION

MIKE BONNER

CHELSEA HOUSE PUBLISHERS

Philadelphia

Produced by Choptank Syndicate, Inc. and Chestnut Productions

Senior Editor: Norman L. Macht
Editor and Picture Researcher: Mary E. Hull
Design and Production: Lisa Hochstein
Cover Illustrator: Cliff Spohn

Project Editor: Jim McAvoy
Art Direction: Sara Davis
Cover Design: Keith Trego

First Printing

1 3 5 7 9 8 6 4 2

Library of Congress Cataloging-in-Publication Data

Bonner, Mike.
    The composite guide to strongman competition / by Mike Bonner.
        p. cm.
    Includes bibliographical references and index.
    ISBN 0-7910-5868-9 (hard)
    1. Weightlifting—Competitions—History. 2. Strong men—History.
I. Title: Strongman competition. II. Title.
GV546.3. .B65 2000
                                                    00-021258

CONTENTS

1   MODERN SAMSONS

Finnish strongman Juoko Ahola picked up two huge 240-pound logs, one in each hand. The logs had handles attached for easy gripping. Ahola held the logs as if they were a pair of light suitcases. He carried them swiftly across a field at the August 15, 1998, Holly, Michigan, Renaissance Festival. A crowd of 18,000 spectators watched eagerly as Ahola covered ground with the two enormous logs at his sides.

This event, known as the farmer's walk, was the first of eight grueling tests of strength to be conducted at the T.G.I. Friday's International Strongman Competition, held as part of the festival. The exciting competition among the modern Samsons rewarded festival promoters with the largest crowd in years.

Master of ceremonies at the T.G.I. Friday's contest was strength sport superstar Magnus Ver Magnusson, four-time World's Strongest Man winner. Microphone in hand, Ver Magnusson provided amusing commentary and kept the various events flowing smoothly. Between events, Ver Magnusson had the crowd laughing with his jokes and antics.

Six competitors were entered in the two-day competition. Points were awarded by standings in each event, ranging from one to six. The first place finisher earned six points, the second place finisher got five points, and so forth.

Although he is physically smaller than many other strongmen, Finnish competitor Juoko Ahola, shown executing the overhead log press, has won two World's Strongest Man titles.

The hot summer sun beat down on Ahola's rippling muscles as he gingerly took one step after another, hefting the nearly 500 pounds of logs. By the time Ahola finally put the logs down, he had outdistanced the other competitors by a large margin, picking up the full six points and the early lead. Those watching noticed that the compact, powerful Ahola hardly seemed winded as he smiled and posed for pictures afterward.

Although Ahola was physically smaller than the other five contestants, he had won the sport's premier competition in 1997, earning the hotly contested World's Strongest Man title. Ahola's handsome face and toothy smile were an attractive accompaniment to his nearly perfect physique. Hailing from Hameenlinna, Finland, Ahola is one of the strongest men in a land of unusually strong men.

At the Renaissance Festival, Ahola's performance in the farmer's walk clearly made him the man to beat.

A typical strongman competition normally consists of six events; the Renaissance Festival competition included eight. Taking place over the entire weekend, the T.G.I. Friday's test of strength and fortitude was in keeping with the spirit of the festival.

Worldwide, dozens of different individual strongman events have been established so far. They include traditional tests of strength like stone lifts, dead lifts, log throws, tugs-of-war, squats, presses, and unique inventions such as car lifts and boat pulls. The most popular events are adapted from traditional contests such as the Scottish Highland Games and the Basque festivals of Spain. Since 1977, the

World's Strongest Man (WSM) competition has been conducted annually at various locations around the world. Strongman competition is a booming sport.

Four countries supply most of the top competitors: Iceland, Britain, South Africa, and Finland. Though small in population, Iceland was originally settled by fearsome Norse raiders. The descendants of these hardy adventurers, such as Icelandic natives Magnus Ver Magnusson and Jon Pall Sigmarsson, have exerted a dominant influence over the strongman sport. The tiny Scandinavian nation of Finland, with only 5.1 million people, likewise fields a collection of high-caliber contenders.

Next up in the Holly, Michigan, International Strongman Competition was the

In the crucifix event, contestants extend their arms and must hold weights that are hung from them. This version is a hold-for-time event, meaning that the instant the contestant's arms begin to sag, the watch stops.

punishing event known as the crucifix. In each hand competitors were required to hold 30-pound sacks of sand straight out from the shoulders for as long as they could. The instant the horizontal plane is broken, the watch stops. Once again, Ahola beat the pack with a time of 65.506 seconds. In second place behind Ahola was the Lumbee Indian chief Harold "Iron Bear" Collins, with a time of 56.22. Third place went to the 6' 5" 360-pound mustachioed German, Heinz Ollesch. A rising star on the international strongman circuit, Ollesch combined tremendous explosive power with outstanding endurance. Another American, Gary Mitchell, tallied fourth to win three points.

In the toss for height event, Ollesch's explosive power really paid off. In the Scottish Games, this event is called the caber toss, or pole toss. A young tree trunk is selected as the throwing device. Ollesch cleared the 16-foot mark with a 48-pound log, easily beating the second place contestant, South African Wayne Price. Ahola took third and earned four points.

The final event of August 15 was a log lift competition, using natural log weights. Starting at about 260 pounds, the competitors each gave it a go. Weights rose rapidly until they hit 320 pounds, at which point competitor Joe DeAngeles dropped out. Massive 365-pound strongman "Iron Bear" Collins won the event with an astonishing 360-pound press, an amount nearly equal to his own weight.

The standings after Saturday's first four strongman events were:

Juoko Ahola—19
Heinz Ollesch—18

Wayne Price—15
"Iron Bear" Collins—14.5
Gary Mitchell—11.5
Joe DeAngeles—6.

On August 16 the competition resumed. Gary Mitchell won the hand-over-hand pull event, in which contestants pull a massive weight toward themselves with a rope. Mitchell's amazing pull lasted 34.38 seconds. The charismatic German, Heinz Ollesch, came in a hair under Mitchell with a time of 34.43 seconds, followed by Ahola at 34.53. After the pull, the spectators marveled at the closeness of an event which saw the first three finishers separated by a mere 15 hundredths of a second.

An event unique to the Renaissance Festival competition was the hay bale push. This event required the competitors to roll awkward 800-pound hay bales along a set course, a variation on the usual car-rolling event, where competitors roll junked cars over a set course. In the hay bale push, the barrel-chested Wayne Price used his low center of gravity to great advantage. Price rolled his bale over the course in 29.84 seconds to win.

Egged on by announcer Ver Magnusson, everybody got a good laugh at the expense of Gary Mitchell. The American competitor suddenly found himself buried face down on the ground when his hay bale collapsed on top of him. Mitchell had to submarine his way out of the straw.

In the stones of strength contest, a variation on a traditional Scottish Games event using special McGlashen stones, competitors had to place huge, smoothly-rounded rocks on top of chest-high barrels, one after the other. Juoko Ahola crowned the barrels in 18.22 seconds, a feat that made the crowd cheer. Earlier, Wayne Price had been on track with an excellent time, but he faltered on the final stone to finish third.

The last event was the wagon dead lift. Heinz Ollesch still had a chance to win, as he trailed Ahola by only three points. The competitors had to raise a wagon loaded with weight. More weight was added as each strongman got the wagon off the ground. But once the weight reached 2,450 pounds, Joe DeAngeles broke the equipment beyond repair. Officials decided to score the event from the last heat, awarding Ahola the overall victory at 38 points.

The 1998 T.G.I. Friday's International Strongman Competition was in most respects a typical outing in this entertaining new sport. While basic strength is absolutely necessary,

In this hand-over-hand pull event, part of the Strongest Man Alive contest, a contestant pulls a Humvee (a broad full-metal military vehicle) toward himself using a rope.

explosive power, flexibility, and endurance are also crucial. The pushing and pulling of various objects demands exertion from a broad range of muscle groups. In many cases, specialized training is required to excel at strongman competition's highest levels. Recent experience has shown that heavyweight bodybuilders and powerlifters are especially successful in strongman competition. Some believe it is because of their superior aerobic capacities.

During the 1980s, American Bill Kazmaier and Icelander Jon Pall Sigmarsson were the sport's most successful competitors. In the 1990s, Magnus Ver Magnusson won four world titles: 1991, 1994, 1995, and 1996. Winners in the sport have usually been exceptionally large men, standing at least 6' 4" and weighing 300 pounds or more.

But Juoko Ahola proved that the biggest strongman wasn't necessarily the best. Despite being the smallest of the six competitors at the 1998 International Strongman Competition, Ahola showed that he was a dominant strongman contender.

Along with strongman competitions, other strength sports gained popularity. At the close of the millennium, weight lifting, powerlifting, bodybuilding, the Scottish Games, and arm wrestling all drew enthusiastic crowds at major events. Champions of these strength sports sometimes gained enough celebrity to appear in movies and on television.

2 ORIGINS OF THE SPORT

The growing popularity of strength sports reminds us of the enduring fascination human beings have had with physical power. From the earliest times, stories and legends abound of heroes who could perform feats of strength far beyond the ability of ordinary mortals.

The Bible story of Samson devotes itself to the life of a long-haired Hebrew strongman whose legend is remarkable for a series of unforgettable exploits. Classical Greek myths focusing on the hero Hercules tell how he completed 12 difficult chores in the service of mankind, including the slaying of a seven-headed serpent, the capture of a swift-footed stag, and the cleaning out of the Augean stables.

To this day, the names Samson and Hercules are associated with feats of strength. The Greeks thought so highly of Hercules that they appointed him god of all athletic contests. In the present era we still have our mythical strongman heroes. The best known is probably Superman, an alien from Krypton. Superman finds such strength in the yellow sun of Earth that he can bend steel with his bare hands, go faster than a speeding bullet, and is able to leap tall buildings in a single bound.

Throughout history, the truest champion of the tribe or nation has always been the biggest and strongest young warrior. This ageless interest in strength provides the driving force for the

Known as "the World's Most Perfectly Developed Man," Charles Atlas, center, became famous for his bodybuilding techniques and his mail-order courses in "dynamic tension," which were supposed to help even the puniest person achieve great muscles.

modern sport of strongman competition. Spectators flock to see hulking men lift rocks, logs, kegs, cars, and massive free weights. They watch enthralled as the strongmen push, pull, and drag wagons, trucks, boats, and even airplanes. People enjoy strength sports because it is fun to imagine oneself doing the same thing.

In recent years strength sports have begun to attract more women. Female competitors such as Connie Price-Smith and Shannon Hartnett have had great success in Scottish Games competitions. Hartnett in particular has been successful, operating a fitness salon while capturing the North American Scottish Games women's records in the light hammer, heavy hammer, and weight toss for height events.

Modern strongman competition is a direct descendant from the Scottish Games, which originated in Scotland during the 11th century. The flamboyant Scottish patriot William Wallace, known as "Braveheart," used the games as a recruiting tool in his wars for Scottish independence. Wallace put winners of the games on the front line in his battles against the English, a duty that was considered a high honor. Today, Scottish Games competitions take place throughout North America and Europe, usually during the summer. The games have a wide following and attract large crowds to outdoor festivals sponsored by towns and cities.

Other than the Scottish Games, modern strength sports have their origins in stage and circus exhibitions. Circus strongmen have been amazing onlookers for hundreds of years.

But throughout the history of Western culture, sports and physical activities were long regarded as unsuited to adults. Until the late 19th century, adults were expected to work at serious jobs and professions. It wasn't considered responsible for adults to be overly concerned with their bodies, bodybuilding, or physical prowess.

A number of social changes in the years before World War I helped alter this perception. The Young Men's Christian Association (YMCA) movement appeared on the scene in 1844, encouraging interest in exercise as an alternative to the unhealthy living conditions in big cities. The increased leisure time afforded people by industrial activity also provided opportunities for them to do things besides work at their jobs.

With perceptions changing, physical work led to physical play. Today, places where strongman competitions are most popular are places where there is a history of hard physical work among the residents. Areas containing existing and former logging camps, mines, docks, farming, grazing, animal husbandry, or similar occupations take especially well to strongman competition.

Meanwhile, the science of bodybuilding gathered momentum during the late 19th century. Pioneer bodybuilders Eugen Sandow, Omer De Bouillion, Wladek Zbyszko, George Hackenschmidt, Walter Godolak, Earle Liederman, and many others became famous for their physical strength. By the 1920s, new magazines like *Physical Culture* and *Muscle Builder* were touting weight training as a way for boys and young men to develop strength,

In the late 1800s, European-born strongman Eugen Sandow traveled in vaudeville shows in the United States, amazing audiences by lifting 19 people and a dog on a board that rested on the back of his neck. In 1893 he appeared at the Chicago World's Fair, where he was touted as "the Strongest Man in the World."

endurance, skill, and self-confidence. During the 1920s, Earle Liederman offered a correspondence course in strength development that was remarkably modern in the quality of its advice and the scope of its program.

Later, a bodybuilder calling himself Charles Atlas produced another version of the Liederman program. The Atlas secret was "dynamic tension," a form of isometric exercise. Atlas advertised his bodybuilding techniques in magazines and comic books from the 1930s through the 1970s. In his ads, Atlas promised to make imposing strength athletes out of 97-pound weaklings. The purpose of the Atlas program was twofold: graduates would develop bodies capable of impressing girls and they could prevent bullies from kicking sand in their faces during beach excursions.

Following in the footsteps of Liederman and Atlas were brothers Joe and Ben Weider. The pair founded a magazine empire based on bodybuilding and strength principles and created the Mr. Olympia competition for the best bodybuilder. They also formed a partnership with famed Austrian bodybuilder Arnold Schwarzenegger in the 1960s. Not surprisingly, Schwarzenegger was the winner of most of the Mr. Olympia contests during his years as a contestant.

One of the most influential bodybuilders and strength athletes of all time was Eugen Sandow. Starting his career as a sideshow strongman, Sandow built himself up to resemble classical Greek and Roman sculptures. In 1899, at the age of 32, Sandow stood 5' 9" tall and weighed 180 pounds. He had a 49" chest, biceps measuring 18", a 36" waist, and 25" thighs. Despite being an almost perfect physical specimen, Sandow wasn't satisfied with being a mere sideshow attraction. He eventually convinced theater producer Flo Ziegfeld to stage an act called "Sandow's Trocadero Vaudevilles" that held audiences rapt with his unique combination of strength, grace, and form.

In many respects, Sandow was way ahead of his time. He was a strongman and a reformer. Along with his lifelong companion, Martinus Sieveking, Sandow advocated physical education in schools, improved urban sanitation, prenatal care for women, and free meals for poor children. Sandow is still so highly regarded in the bodybuilding community that his image graces the statuette awarded to the annual winner of the Mr. Olympia contest, bodybuilding's top event.

Although strength sports have been around for thousands of years, modern strongman competition began in 1977. That year Universal TV Studios rolled out the first World's Strongest Man competition, or WSM, as it is has come to be called. The concept was seen initially as a gimmick television program. The first WSM was filmed in three successive days of competition. Later, the program's events were shown on consecutive Saturdays during the 1977–78 television season.

Except for one year, a World's Strongest Man competition has been held annually since 1977. The sport is exceptionally popular in the United Kingdom. Every year, about 33 million Britons turn on their TVs to watch the WSM competition. A company named Trans World International produces the World's Strongest Man contest for the BBC and other networks.

Producers of the original broadcast contacted Oscar State, the secretary of the International Weightlifting Federation (IWF), for expert advice. State in turn called on his friend David Webster, an influential figure in British strength sports, for information and competitor recommendations. A renowned weight lifter, Webster had extensive coaching experience and officiated at many World and European Championships and Olympic Games.

At the time, Webster was organizing Scottish Games on a professional basis with another strength sports advocate, Dr. Douglas Edmunds. Webster brought Edmunds in on the development of the program and together the men formed a long association with the World's Strongest Man competition.

Between 1964 and 1968, Douglas Edmunds was a shot put and discus champion. In 1976 and 1978, Edmunds won the World Professional Caber Toss. Edmunds also won the prestigious Braemar Highland Games in 1976. Given his extensive background in strength sports, it was only natural for Edmunds to put his organizing abilities to work on behalf of strongman events.

Initially, the organizing group for strongman competition was called the World Federation of International Heavy Events Athletes. Records show that David Webster registered a claim to the concept in 1973. The consolidation of the strongman sport led the organization to become known as the International Federation of Strength Athletes (IFSA). The IFSA functions as the governing body for the sport of strongman competition.

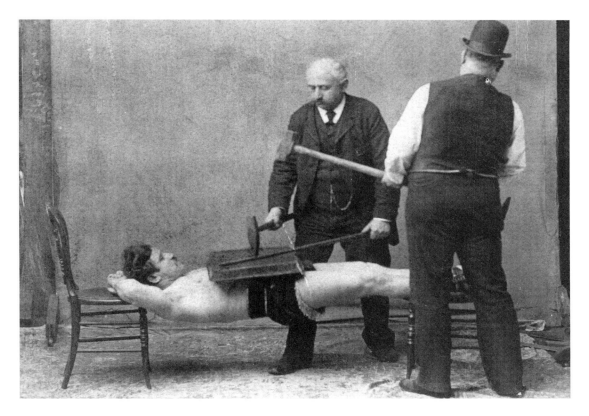

Modern strongman competition has been tirelessly promoted by Edmunds, president and founder of the IFSA. The best-known strongman competitions are those sanctioned by the IFSA. During the past quarter century, the IFSA has overseen the development of better training and competition, which in turn has led to the participation of more skilled athletes.

Because it resembles the Scottish Games in events like the weight toss and strength stones, strongman competition owes much of its vitality to the traditional Scottish Games. But strongman competition also prides itself on being a little different.

Early 20th century strongman Ivan Skobel amazed audiences with his feats of strength. Using his muscles to keep his body taut, Skobel lies stretched out between two chairs while two men beat on his stomach with sledgehammers.

Drawing on the old notion of showing off in the village square, strongman competition is open to locally-flavored, unique tests of power. From the beginning, Webster and Edmunds devised challenges for larger audiences than the Scottish Games normally attract. The most significant among their innovations are the strength stones, or McGlashen stones, so named in honor of the original masons who crafted them. Patterned after the Braemar stones, the oldest continuous event in the Scottish Games, this may be the purest test of overall human power ever invented. Each stone is a perfectly round rock. The smallest weighs 198 pounds. Competitors place the stones on top of barrels, one after the other, as the crowd cheers its favorites. Try to imagine hoisting a 200-pound bowling ball atop a four foot tall rack; it's the same idea. The combination of movements—lifting, running from stone to stone, struggling with the heaviest stone—rouses spectators like nothing else.

Two-time Olympic gold medal winner Vasily Alexeyev attempts to lift 528 lbs. during the clean and jerk lift at the World Weight Lifting Championship held at Gettysburg College on October 9, 1978. Alexeyev pulled a right hip tendon while attempting this lift and had to drop the weights.

The 1970s were a time of great interest in strength sports. Movies like *Pumping Iron* brought thousands of people into health clubs, and bodybuilding became a national craze. Strength sports got another boost in the mid-1970s when the Russian weight lifter Vasily Alexeyev dominated his sport by setting 80 world records and winning two Olympic gold medals.

Alexeyev's most dramatic moment came at the Montreal Olympics in 1976. German opponent Gerd Bonk had broken Alexeyev's old record in the clean and jerk by lifting 557 pounds. In lifting 557 pounds, Bonk had issued his greatest challenge to Alexeyev. Now it was the Russian's turn to lift. Alexeyev strode to the platform with his usual slow, stately march. Once there, he ordered new weights added to the bar, bringing the total to 562 pounds. Alexeyev stared at the steel barbells, all 562 pounds of them. It would be a world record if he could pull it off. The tension was almost unbearable.

With a mighty grunt, Alexeyev got under the bar. Using every ounce of his power, Alexeyev brought it to his shoulders, staggered briefly, and then raised the weight high overhead as the crowd shouted his name to the rafters.

Alexeyev brought worldwide attention to his sport with his weight lifting feats in the late 1970s. His astounding performance in the 1976 Montreal Olympics encouraged additional strength contests. Soon strongman competition became a main attraction in the strength sport menu.

FEATS OF STRENGTH

Strongman competition is a hybrid sport, and it has absorbed events and athletes from more established contests. Other strength sports supply most of its best contestants. Most notably, weight lifting, powerlifting, bodybuilding, and the Scottish Games funnel contestants to strongman competition at every level. Other sports like discus, shot put, the Olympic hammer, and arm wrestling demonstrate potential for making contributions to strongman competition.

As might be expected, many different strength athletes can compete successfully in strongman competitions. The combination of skills needed—explosive power, flexibility, endurance, and general body strength—are characteristic of all kinds of strength athletes.

Interest in strength and fitness is increasing nationally. Strongman competition below the WSM level is flourishing in many parts of the world, especially in Europe. The booming interest in strength sports has people looking for ways to get in on the action. As a consequence, strongman competition isn't the only strength sport currently gaining in popularity. The whole range of strength sports is currently laying claim to the attention of many novice competitors.

Women are also moving into strength competition. Since passage of Title IX of the 1972 U.S. Civil Rights Act, women have been encouraged to participate in competitive sports. Title IX

Nigerian weight lifter Franca Gbodo lifts 187 lbs. to win the snatch event at the All-Africa Games in 1999. In the snatch event, weight lifters hoist the barbell up to chest level in one quick motion, then stand erect with the bar overhead and their arms straight. Weight lifting and powerlifting are two strength sports in which women excel.

Dressed in Scotch plaid, a strongman competitor uses all of his might to complete the caber toss, a traditional Scottish Games event.

mandated equity in college sports programs. This means that colleges must provide as many sports opportunities for women as they do for men.

Despite the fact that nature seems to have endowed men with a slightly larger base on which to build muscle, many women have achieved stunning muscular development. Chinese women own most of the Olympic weight lifting records. American women have also turned in many outstanding efforts in the national and international strength realms.

At the USA Women's National Powerlifting Championships held in February of 1999, heavyweight competitors Leslie Look and Liz Willet racked up scores of 530 and 492.5 kilograms respectively. This means the women brought up over 1,000 pounds in their three top powerlifts. Powerlifting is scored by the best lift in all three categories to produce a combined final score.

In weight lifting, female stars like Lea Foreman are turning in lifts that compare favorably with the best that men can do, pound for pound. Both genders are making headway in modern strength sports, and the science of physical development is advancing rapidly.

To an outsider, the most obvious difference between weight lifting and powerlifting is that each sport has its own lifts. Otherwise, they both use a bar to raise iron dumbbells from a platform. Weight lifting has two lifts: the snatch and the clean and jerk. Powerlifting has three lifts: the squat, the press, and the dead lift. Each sport subscribes to a somewhat different philosophy. Weight lifting is ancient, going back some 3,000 years. Powerlifting is more modern, with a looser structure and more emphasis on individual style. The sport of powerlifting made itself felt in strongman competition when a pioneer powerlifter, Don Reinhoudt, won the 1979 WSM title.

Powerlifting is not an Olympic event. For a time, the press qualified as an Olympic lift, but it was discontinued in 1972. Instead, amateur powerlifters worldwide compete in events sanctioned by the International Powerlifting Federation (IPF).

In weight lifting, competitors have refined the snatch to a high degree of sophistication; it is an explosive lift, done in one fluid motion. In the snatch, the lifter pulls the weighted bar up from the platform. As it rises to chest level, the lifter drops into a squatting position, with the bar overhead and arms straight. The lifter then must stand erect.

The clean and jerk generally involves much heavier weights than the snatch. An exceptionally difficult lift when performed at the highest level, the clean and jerk is the most exciting of all lifts. It differs from the snatch in several respects. Instead of going immediately into the squat, the bar is brought up to the lifter's thighs. The lifter uses the thighs to drive the bar upward, receiving it on the shoulders before going into the squat. Once the bar is on the shoulders, the lifter dips and drives the bar upward in an explosive effort to raise it overhead. Coaches train their lifters on safe ways to get out from under the bar if the lift isn't going to work.

Powerlifting is similar to weight lifting but relies on different styles and techniques. In the powerlift known as the squat, the lifter takes the bar from a pair of squat stands, holds it behind the head, drops to a squatting position, and then stands back up. In the press, a bar is held across the chest while the lifter reclines on a bench. When the official gives the signal, the lifter raises the bar so that the arms are straight. In the dead lift, enormous weights are brought up from the platform to a level just below the waist. Lifting a car or wagon by its bumper is a good example of a dead lift. In powerlifting, the dead lift is always done with weighted bars. Strongman competitions include dead lifts with all kinds of things besides weighted bars.

The Scottish Games steer many competitors toward strongman sports. These ancient tests of strength and skill enjoy enduring popularity. Fans can expect to see kilted men and women facing off in Scottish Games as a bagpipe begins to play. The events that constitute the Scottish Games are the light and heavy stones, the weight for distance, and the light and heavy hammer, sheaf, and weight tosses. Scottish Games athletes who become competitors in strongman events arrive with a good foundation on which to build. The ingredients for success in Scottish Heavy Events—power, flexibility, practice, observation, experimentation, and body control—are the same ones that spell success in strongman.

Another fascinating strength sport is arm wrestling. No successful armsports competitor has yet broken into strongman, but it is a possibility. The sport claims over 300 professionals,

with national contests on a weekly basis. The prizes in the biggest events top $50,000.

Organized arm wrestling started as a saloon sport in the 1950s. Tavern bouncers in the town of Petaluma, California, got together to see which one was the strongest. Since that small beginning, arm wrestling has become a national passion and has been televised worldwide. A formal organization was established by sport founders Bill Soberanes and Dave Devoto to oversee the competitions. The late *Peanuts* cartoonist Charles Schulz gave arm wrestling a boost when the dog Snoopy became interested in the sport. Sadly, Snoopy was disqualified from competition when it was discovered that, as a canine, he had no thumbs.

At the October 1999 USA Arm Wrestling Championships, the participants competed in gender, weight, and age classes in left-handed and right-handed events. Eric Woelfel won the Pro-Men's left in the heavyweight class; Vakhtang Javakhadse won the Pro-Men's right. In the women's division, Theresa Ebert

The tug-of-war, performed by Irish teams during an Irish heritage festival in Milwaukee, Wisconsin, is one of the many traditional strength competitions celebrated in Celtic culture.

Contestants Roy Maurer, left, and Frank Malis compete in the 1998 Golden Arm Championship sponsored by the New York Arm Wrestling Association. Arm wrestling is one of the most popular strength sports in the United States.

walked away with the Pro-Ladies left, and Sherry Mundy won the Pro-Ladies right.

Strongman competition has adapted many heavyweight strength events to suit its purposes. Although bodybuilders make superior strongman competitors, the muscular body shape resulting from disciplined physical development is of less value than pure strength. Modern strongman competition owes much of the excitement it has generated to the spontaneous nature of its events, which are less structured than those involved in Olympic weight lifting, powerlifting, and Scottish Games.

Today's lifters, strength athletes, and bodybuilders have inherited their sports from pioneers such as Sandow, Liederman, Atlas,

Webster, the Weiders, Alexeyev, and many others. These pioneers saw a future for physical development that would not just improve the body, but also the mind and spirit. Scientific advancement in nutrition and exercise developed by strength competitors are beneficial to ordinary people as well.

If there is a major drawback to organized strongman competition, it is the lack of women at the sport's highest level. The year 1999 saw no women's equivalent to the World's Strongest Man contest. The Scottish Games, on the other hand, have been a leader in accepting women into the sport. Exciting stars like Shannon Hartnett and Connie Price-Smith are setting records in the North American Scottish Games that will be tough to beat. The lack of women in the WSM is an oversight that needs to be corrected before the sport can advance.

An influential international strongman advocate, Manfred Hoeberl, recently won election as an IFSA vice-president. Hoeberl expressed hope that an equivalent WSM competition for women would soon arise.

"We want to have team events, and I want to have women's events," Hoeberl said. "So it's not going to be [just] the strongest and the biggest guy. We're going to have height classes, hopefully. This will still take a while."

4 MAKING MUSCLE

Training to be a strongman contender takes a lot of hard work. More than that, though, there must be an intense desire to excel. Obstacles to success are immense. To succeed at strongman, competitors must train properly, nourish themselves well, have a good attitude, and be prepared to devote many long hours to the sport.

The type of body needed to win at international strongman competition is not well distributed among the world's population. In a world where many go hungry, heavyweight Goliaths from six-and-a-half to seven-feet tall, weighing about 300 to 350 pounds, are relatively rare. The attraction of strongman competition is the chance to see the biggest and strongest do what they do best: flex their muscles and show their power.

Given the basic material, structured training regimens and nutritional programs will help develop what nature has provided. Exercise and disciplined routines recommended by experts provide professional strongmen with the competitive edge they need to succeed.

But there are limits to what the human body can do by itself. Nineteenth century pioneer bodybuilders like Eugen Sandow, using scientific methods, were thought to have pushed normal human bodies about as far as they could go. Then the rapid development of new steroid drugs in the years following World War II allowed

Using brute force and will, a strongman competitor smashes his elbow through a pile of cinder blocks, breaking them in half.

certain European and Russian weight lifters to shatter records as never before. By 1964, nearly all the steroid drugs commonly used today had been synthesized. Chief among them was a drug marketed under the name Dianabol, a synthetic form of the male hormone testosterone. A naturally-occurring substance, testosterone encourages the body to produce muscle from the raw materials in food. Once the body absorbs synthetic testosterone, it makes more muscle than would normally occur through exercise. Not even the most strenuous and time-consuming exercises will produce the results gained by the use of steroids. The use of performance-enhancing drugs, or PEDs, as they are called, was banned by the International Olympic Committee (IOC) in 1974. However, they still remain a major problem in strength sports and other professional sports.

Recent estimates suggest that perhaps two-thirds of strength athletes use, or have used, PEDs. In an October 1999 article in *Thorax's Iron Magazine*, a publication dedicated to strength sports, writer Chris Thibaudeau concluded that steroids had tainted strength sports to the extent that serious competitors might not be able to win without using them occasionally.

"We have to be realists, though; it is almost impossible to be an Olympic or World champion without ever taking PED," Thibaudeau wrote.

At the professional level, testing for substance abuse varies from sport to sport. In the United States, organized powerlifting goes so far as to call itself the "Drug Free Powerlifting Association" and has extensive testing programs for athletes. The toughest testing occurs under IOC rules. To inform athletes about banned substances, the IOC has established a toll-free hotline number [1 (800) 233-0393] which advises them about what is allowed and what is not.

North American Scottish Games Association (NASGA) competition, a close relative to American strongman competition, faithfully subscribes to IOC rules and testing. NASGA adheres to procedures laid down by the IOC.

Strongman Karl Dodge, a Scottish Games competitor from Colorado, refuses to use substances that enhance his competitive abilities. Dodge disapproves of international strongman competition because he believes imany of the athletes rely on illegal substances to improve their performance.

"One of my values as an athlete is not to use performance-enhancing drugs, and I simply refuse to do that to myself and my body," Dodge said. "I want to maintain my integrity as an athlete. In order to compete in the World's Strongest Man you have to use performance-enhancing drugs; most people can't do those things naturally. There is maybe one out of 10 WSM competitors who doesn't use them. And that's why I don't do it and enjoy my sport."

Ironically, so many legal products are being sold to improve athletic performance that even conscientious competitors like Dodge can sometimes get into trouble. During the 1998 Costa Mesa Highland Games in Costa Mesa, California, Dodge drank an over-the-counter orange-flavored liquid commonly found at nutrition stores. As a result, he had to explain

A strongman competitor attempts to hoist a stone onto the platform. One of the most excruciating events in modern-day strongman competition, the stones of strength event is based on a strength game that originated over 1,000 years ago in Scotland.

the presence of the drug ephedrine in his body. It wasn't easy. Dodge's apology letter read in part:

"Discovering my mistake was very embarrassing. I have always been an active advocate of competing drug-free and would never risk my integrity as a professional athlete by taking something that would give me an advantage over any fellow professional athletes and result in a ban from the sport that I love so much."

Besides the unfairness steroid use brings to competition, use of these products can also have severe negative health effects. Steriod use can cause liver cancer, male breast enlargement, and increased aggressive behaviors. Aggressive behaviors caused by steroids are known collectively as " 'roid rage" among athletes. Athletes who use steroids in sport are not only cheating others, they are cheating themselves.

Beginners interested in making muscle are advised to stay away from illegal substances. Adolescent development can be seriously hampered by steroids. Instead, a muscle-building program like the basic 3–1–3 training regimen is recommended for novices.

The 3–1–3 program works like this: Divide your body into three workout areas, rest one day, and then repeat. On the first day, exercise to build chest, shoulders, and abdominals. On the second day, work on legs and calves. Day three will be devoted to arms and back muscles. The day off in the middle gives the body the rest it needs to grow.

People familiar with strength sports recommend that beginners use free weights instead of machines. Using free weights is easier on growing joints and helps get the muscle builder acquainted with the touch and feel of lifting iron. Both powerlifting and weight lifting use free weights in their events. Many books available at school and public libraries provide information on the effective use of free weights in building muscles.

Strongman competitors have different, personalized training regimens. German strongman Heinz Ollesch says he goes mostly by instinct in his training.

"I train four times a week," Ollesch has said, "but I don't have a training plan. I train [by] my feelings."

Other athletes suggest that competitors get to know their bodies generally. An interview

Strapped into a special harness, 57-year-old strongman contestant Gerard J. Baril pulls a Humvee for 45 yards at the third annual Brooklyn Fair Strongman Competition held in Brooklyn, Connecticut, on August 29, 1998.

between Austrian strongman Manfred Hoeberl and Bill Henderson, author of the *World's Strongest Man* official homepage, revealed that Hoeberl approaches his sport scientifically. Henderson said he was impressed by how much Hoeberl knew about how the human body works.

"Well, it seems if you're a professional, I think it's something you need to have," Hoeberl said. "Like, I could never accept if you're an auto mechanic and you don't know about a car."

Hoeberl opposes performance-enhancing drug use by strongman competitors. As a newly installed vice president of the IFSA in 1998, Hoeberl said he welcomed steroid testing for strongman athletes.

"In Australia in April [1999], we are having an IOC test for the first time ever for our athletes," Hoeberl said in 1998. "Which is a little heavier, I think, for now because we have to give them time to get the right direction. But, we're going to try it and I fully support that."

As professional athletes discover more ways to enhance physical strength with drugs, the use of such substances expands. In some cases, it can be hard to tell the difference between a drug and a legal product. Although the substance creatine resembles some banned products, it is also a natural chemical produced in the kidneys and liver, so the IOC has not included creatine on its banned substance list.

Strongman competition around the world closely follows its cousin in strength sports, the Scottish Games athletic competitions. Competitors move back and forth between the two sports, although the use of performance-enhancing drugs is more heavily regulated in the Scottish Games than it is in strongman competition. Rules for PED usage among Scottish Games competitors are IOC rules, which (as previously stated) maintain an extensive list of banned substances.

All around the world, the strongest of the strong face off in stirring contests, but the permitted usage of PEDs undermines the integrity of the sport. To clean up the sport, organizers like former competitor Manfred Hoeberl are urging the widespread adoption of IOC rules and testing. Everyone concerned with the future of strongman competition sincerely hopes they succeed.

5

STRONGMAN CONTEST HISTORY

Strongman competition has established a devoted following around the world and a knowledgeable fan base. The development of the sport has been linked to that first televised *World's Strongest Man* broadcast back in 1977. To encourage interest in the original TV program, producers David Webster and Douglas Edmunds sought athletes who, like themselves, had established reputations in strength sports and professional athletics.

The producers had two goals in mind for the first WSM competition. First, they wanted to line up a crew of top quality athletes and put them through a series of grueling tests. They hoped the tests would give the winner a legitimate claim to being the World's Strongest Man. Second, they wanted to put on an entertaining show that would draw viewers.

While the television cameras rolled, the inaugural battle for the title of World's Strongest Man got under way. Eight top-notch athletes battled through 10 events in three days to produce a winner. Heavyweight Olympic lifter Bruce Wilhelm won the 1977 competition, scoring 63.25 points, 20 points ahead of Bob Young, his next closest opponent. At the time, Young played offensive tackle for the St. Louis (now Arizona) Cardinals of the National Football League. Behind Young in third place was another Olympian, weight lifter Ken Patera.

In the trap bar hold-for-time event, a Strongest Man Alive contestant holds two weighted safes off the ground.

Fourth place went to Lou Ferrigno, who is best known to TV audiences for his role on the program *The Incredible Hulk*. Ferrigno is a good example of a strength competitor who turned his athletic prominence into a successful show business career. Arnold Schwarzenegger, star of the *Terminator* movies, *Kindergarten Cop*, and other films, is another example of the strongman-to-actor progression.

Wilhelm grabbed the first WSM victory by winning five of the 10 events, including the barrel lift, the wheelbarrow race, the tug-of-war, the trolley pull, and the refrigerator race. Only one other competitor, Ferrigno, came out on top in more than one of the events. Ferrigno placed first in the bar bend and the car lift.

Following that first successful *World's Strongest Man* TV show in 1977, interest in the sport blossomed. Strongman contests were held outside the United States. The entire continent of Europe had sent only one athlete to the WSM in 1977—Franco Columbu, an Italian. Columbu placed fifth in the first WSM, not a bad showing for a token invitee. The next year, 1978, nations outside the United States sent three athletes to the WSM competition—Lars Hedlund of Sweden, Israeli Boris Djerassi, and the Polish heavyweight Ivan Putski. Since then the United States has fielded a minority of the WSM competitors. In the years 1994, 1996, and 1999, no American athletes reached the finals.

The success of the *World's Strongest Man* show surprised the TV producers and led to the planning of a sequel the following year. Since its 1977 debut, strongman competition has come a long way, assuming its current spot at the forefront of strength athletics. Strongman competition boasts a broad appeal because it adapts to local conditions and provides the variety of thrills spectators crave.

In the wake of the initial 1977 broadcast, a large influx of athletes, events, and spectator excitement spurred more strongman competition. Weight lifting and other muscle power competitors were encouraged to participate in strongman contests.

Once the World's Strongest Man competition gained steam in the late 1970s, a string of Americans dominated the sport. Wilhelm won again in 1978, although opponents questioned the level of sportsmanship he displayed during his victories.

Particularly dismayed by Wilhelm's badmouthing was Don Reinhoudt, a successful powerlifter who likewise proved he had the stuff to win at strongman competition. Powerlifting translates well to strongman competition because the flexibility and explosiveness

Magnus Ver Magnusson of Iceland, a four-time World's Strongest Man winner, pulls three semitrailers across a parking lot during a Scandinavian heritage festival held in Minot, North Dakota, in 1998. Many strongman competitions feature a truck pull event.

needed to powerlift successfully are valuable strongman attributes. When Reinhoudt defeated Wilhelm in several of the individual events, Wilhelm responded with a series of insults to Reinhoudt.

The 1979 strongman competition saw two European contestants break into the top three spots. Lars Hedlund of Sweden and Geoff Capes of Britain came in just behind Don Reinhoudt.

The World's Strongest Man competition of 1980 witnessed the debut of a truly outstanding athlete in the person of Bill Kazmaier. Although Americans haven't had much success in strongman competitions at the elite level, Kazmaier, an American, is regarded by some as the best strongman competitor ever. There are many who say Kazmaier is perhaps the strongest human being in history.

All agree that Kazmaier was an amazing physical specimen, standing 6' 2" and weighing 320 pounds. Kazmaier's upper arms each measured 22", and his chest puffed out to a full 60" over a trim 40" waist.

He competed in college football and a host of other sports before becoming interested in powerlifting. Kazmaier was junior and senior national powerlifting champ in 1978 and won superheavyweight lifting titles throughout the 1980s. He set strongman records and won the World's Strongest Man title in 1980, '81, and '82. After his third win, the WSM failed to invite Kazmaier back, reportedly to give others a chance.

"They didn't want this guy named Kazmaier to dominate anymore," he said in 1997, "so he was just not invited for five years. Which wasn't because of my own retirement, it was a forced retirement—which is really a shame because Michael Jordan wouldn't be asked to sit on the sidelines. Nor would Wayne Gretzky. It would be a travesty in sport if that would happen, and the fans wouldn't let it happen. But in our sport, it's so small that there are a few people that are in control and they . . . want to manipulate and control and run things. And they've been able to do that."

Despite being snubbed by the WSM organizers after his 1982 win, Kaz was still popular. When strongman fans were recently asked to rate past competitors on the basis of strength, Kaz won again, taking 37 percent of the vote. Magnus Ver Magnusson came in second with 32.4 percent of the vote. John Pall Sigmarsson trailed, a distant third at 9.6 percent.

Removing Kaz from the World's Strongest Man competition opened the doors for other entries. Britain's Geoff Capes, who came in second to Kaz in 1981, snagged the 1983 title with 49.5 points. Then-newcomer Jon Pall Sigmarsson of Iceland finished a razor-thin second place behind Capes with 48, followed by Siem Wulfse of the Netherlands at 47.

The 1984 WSM saw a memorable battle between Sigmarsson and another Dutchman, Ab Wolders. Sigmarsson won with 57.5 points to Wolders's 51.5. Geoff Capes made another run at the 1984 title as well but came in third at 49 points.

In 1985, organizers renamed their parent organization the Federation of International Strength Athletes. Both 1985 and 1986 saw Sigmarsson and his rival Capes duel to the limit. Capes won the 1985 battle, 50.5 to 49, while the great Sigmarsson came out on top in 1986, winning 59 to 55 over Capes. Dutchmen grabbed third place both years: Cees De Vreugd in 1985 and veteran Ab Wolders in 1986.

There was no contest in 1987. Producers of the World's Strongest Man failed to put on an official show, and strongman enthusiasts around the world went without a 1987 victor, TV show, results, or memories.

Things got rolling again in 1988 with a standard issue WSM, held in Hungary. This time Kazmaier was back in the running and gave Sigmarsson his best shot. But Sigmarsson prevailed on the strength of his performances in the loading, the truck pull, the weight for height, and the McGlashen stones events. Kazmaier won all the other 1988 events except for one. Jamie Reeves of the United Kingdom beat everyone in the forward hold, which was good enough for a 47-point third place finish.

Reeves got off to a hot start when the WSM selected Spain as the site for the 1989 contest. He won the log lift, the farmer's walk, the crucifix, and the truck pull, exciting the crowd with his consistency and British bulldog power. Once again Ab Wolders finished in the money, nabbing second place, this time just a nose ahead of Sigmarsson.

In 1990 Jon Pall Sigmarsson bagged his greatest triumph, winning the WSM with 48.5 points, beating out the massive American O. D. Wilson by a mere half-point.

Meanwhile, the nation of Finland, small in population but large in strength, put one of its sons in the top three for the first time in 1990 when Ilkka Nummisto captured third place with 39 points. Nummisto's finish was not the last time the land of reindeer and tundra would place a man among the WSM's top contenders.

The nations of Northern Europe dominated the WSM throughout the 1990s, winning every competition. In 1991 it was Iceland's turn as Magnus Ver Magnusson broke into the top spot, winning with a score of 56 points over

Carrying two 160-pound weights, a strongman contestant performs the farmer's walk, a grueling trip that includes climbing 12" steps over a platform.

Danish star Henning Thorson. British power-lifter Gary Taylor won third.

When the WSM contest set up shop in Iceland during the summer of 1992, a Dutchman named Ted Van Der Parre beat local favorite Magnus Ver Magnusson and Jamie Reeves by a single point.

A French setting was selected for the WSM the next year. Gary Taylor of the U.K. shrugged off his earlier defeat to win the title narrowly over Ver Magnusson, 54-49. The gigantic Finnish strongman Riku Kiri made his first appearance in the top three that year, right behind Ver Magnusson at 48.5 points.

The mid-1990s were the age of Ver Magnusson, as he won the WSM title in 1994, 1995, and 1996. But it was never easy. He had to fend off an exceptionally tough challenge from the Austrian Manfred Hoeberl in 1994, winning 50.5 to 49.5. In 1995 it was the South African Gerrit Badenhorst who went after Ver Magnusson, coming in on the short end of a 71- to 62.5-point finish. The towering Finn Riku Kiri came in second to Ver Magnusson in 1996, losing 53–43. Every year, the top competitors were generally the same. Kiri had also placed third in 1994, as did Badenhorst in 1996. Another Finn, Marko Varalahti, took the second spot in 1995.

In 1995 additional changes to the sport led to yet another name change, with the organization adopting the name by which it is currently known, the International Federation of Strength Athletes (IFSA). Representation by the participating nations is currently managed through a senate body. In cooperation with the Trans World International television production group, the IFSA selects which athletes will appear in the World's Strongest Man competition.

Finland nailed down the WSM outright for the first time in 1997. This win coincided with the emergence of an exciting new star, Juoko Ahola. Scoring 61 points overall, Ahola beat the Dane Flemming Rasmussen by a margin of four points. A dynamic Swedish competitor, Magnus Samuelsson, came in third with 52.5 points.

When the WSM moved to Morocco in 1998, Ahola finished a disappointing second to Samuelsson, 73–67, while still another new star, Dutchman Woudt Zijlstra, came in third.

Despite the occasionally erratic history that strongman competition has seen since its origin, the sport has demonstrated that as long as there are big, strong men, there will be people eager to see what they can do.

THE WORLD'S
STRONGEST MAN

6

After more than two decades of strong-man competition, the sport has more events than ever. The 1999 official IFSA tour featured 23 events, including some, like the June Beauty and the Beast Hawaiian Grand Prix, in which the winner received an invitation to the World's Strongest Man contest.

IFSA events drew crowds on both sides of the Atlantic, selecting the Strongest Man for Scot-land, Spain, Holland, Canada, Hungary, Sweden, and Czechoslovakia, to name a few. American events included strongest man and strongest woman competitions in Texas, Virginia, Penn-sylvania, and California, among many others. Muscle opposed muscle in exciting contests like the annual Buffalo's Strongest Man, the Blue Ridge Strongman/Woman, the California Iron Warrior, and the Strongest Man Alive, which attracted some of the sport's top athletes.

But the premier event in modern strength sports continued to be the World's Strongest Man competition. Fans of strongman consider the WSM the Super Bowl of physical prowess.

The 1999 WSM was held on the island of Malta, located south of Sicily in the Mediterranean Sea. This ancient island nation, first settled by Phoenician traders in 2500 B.C., provided a colorful backdrop to strongman competition's longest-running contest.

In the log lift event strongmen must press a log, or iron bar, over-head. The weights are increased with each round until only one competitor can still press the log.

Competitors from around the world gathered to put their bodies to the test. Top strongman competitions feature qualifying rounds to narrow the field to eight or 10 participants, who then face off in a series of events to determine the winner. Most of the entrants at the WSM were well-known in strength sports circles. Some early favorites emerged from the qualifying rounds to stand out from the pack.

The most obvious candidate for the 1999 WSM title was the Swede Magnus Samuelsson, the winner in 1998. A second potential victor was Juoko Ahola, the 1997 winner and the 1998 runner-up to Samuelsson. Ahola's countryman, Janne Virtanen, also shared the inside track. Noted for his flexibility and speed, Virtanen had run a close third to Ahola at the March 1999 Finnish Grand Prix. Another Finn, Sami Heinonen, had taken the second place spot in the grueling six-event contest. In a boost to Ahola, Heinonen did not make it to the WSM. Instead, Heinonen participated in the Strongman II competition in St. Louis, Missouri, a Children's Miracle Network benefit.

Not to be dismissed at the qualifying was an American, Whit Baskin. At the Beauty and the Beast Challenge in Hawaii, Baskin earned excellent scores in the Hercules hold and the loading event, though he only finished fifth overall. The giant Canadian Hugo Girard and the blond Norwegian superman Svend Karlsen also counted as serious contenders for the 1999 WSM crown.

The qualifying rounds for the 1999 WSM ran September 9–12. Competition producers divided the contestants into five groups. The top two qualifiers in each group would be

A 1998 Strongest Man Alive contestant carries a huge triangle-shaped rock, known as the Husafell or Hanaford stone.

competing in the final rounds. During the qualifiers, the groups faced different events. In the first round, the contestants all participated in a carry and drag. Then the groups split up so that two did a truck pull while the others carried the Husafell stone, a huge triangle-shaped rock.

Juoko Ahola finished first in his group, carrying the 170-kilogram Husafell stone 70 meters. The carry and drag involved loading three heavy objects in a sled and dragging the sled across a finish line. Whit Baskin got off to a good start by winning both the carry and drag as well as the truck pull in his group. Ahola's countryman Janne Virtanen showed his stuff by winning both events in his group as well.

By the third day of the qualifiers, the groups began to sort out more clearly. Magnus Samuelsson led Group One with 21 points. Ahola led Group Two with 22 points. Janne Virtanen led Group Three with a perfect 24 points. Group Four saw Hugo Girard in the lead with 23 points. And Group Five was dominated by Dutch strongman Berend Veneberg with 21 points. On September 12, qualifying came to an end, and the top two competitors in each group moved into the finals.

The 10 finalists were Juoko Ahola, Janne Virtanen, Svend Karlsen, Hugo Girard, Magnus Samuelsson, Berend Veneberg, Torfi Olafson, Jamie Barr, Laszlo Fekete, and Rene Minkfitz. From among these 10 men, the 1999 World's Strongest Man would emerge. Before that happened, though, each man would be put through a series of trying tests of strength.

Two events were held on the first day of the finals. The first competition was called the super yoke. This required the competitors to carry a pair of engine blocks, dangling by chains from a cross bar. Each strongman held the cross bar atop his shoulders and carried the blocks over a short course. The weight of the blocks totaled 355 kilograms, or about 780 pounds. Svend Karlsen won the super yoke, coming in a second faster than Juoko Ahola. Janne Virtanen finished third. The second

With Magnus Ver Magnusson, standing at right, acting as referee, American strongman Whit Baskin, seated right, tries to pull his opponent over the line during the bar pull at the annual Strongest Man Alive contest.

event was a dead lift hold which Ahola won, followed by Karlsen and Veneberg.

Day two saw the men slug it out in three different events. The biggest crowd pleaser was the boat pull. Contestants pulled an empty fishing craft up a steep incline, using a rope to do it in a hand-over-hand motion. Magnus Samuelsson, an Iceland native, won the boat pull. Poor technique kept Juoko Ahola from doing better than fifth in the boat pull, but he said afterward that he was not discouraged.

"I'm not happy with my fifth place but not too disappointed either," Ahola said. "I put everything I got on [the] line. Also there are still events and days left."

The biggest challenge of all faced the competitors on day three of the 1999 WSM. Contest organizers put together an event that required the men to pull a Boeing 737 jet. It was the biggest object ever moved in a WSM contest. In the airplane pull, Ahola came in second behind Virtanen. By placing second in both events,

Ahola scored 18 points. The finish was good enough to put Ahola in first place with only one day remaining in the 1999 WSM.

The competitors put everything on the line as the 1999 WSM moved into its final day. The critical event on that last day was the giant log lift. Hugo Girard beat the others on the giant 121 kilogram log, raising it from his chest overhead 17 times. Magnus Samuelsson came in second, with 15 repetitions. Ahola cemented his hold on first place with 14 reps, finishing third in the event.

The final event was a replay of the carry and drag from the qualifiers. Ahola came in second after Svend Karlsen. Ahola's strong performances overall, even in the events he did not win, gave him the point totals needed for victory.

Janne Virtanen, Ahola's fellow Finn, expressed his pleasure in achieving second place over many more experienced and world-class competitors:

"It tasted sweet and gave me belief for the future. It's good to continue from this," Virtanen said.

For the second time in three years, Juoko Ahola had won the title of the World's Strongest Man. Not since the age of Magnus Ver Magnusson had a competitor won two titles within a three year period.

From Malta the 1999 WSM strongman competitors moved to Panyu, China. The world's largest nation was hosting the world's strongest men in a show that pitted pairs of athletes against each other. To no one's surprise, the Finnish team of Juoko Ahola and Janne Virtanen won the 1999 World Team

Championships before a live crowd of 35,000 and nearly 800 million Chinese TV viewers.

North America and Europe have so far had the best organized and longest-running strongman programs. But the warm 1999 welcome competitors experienced in China during the World Team Championships indicated that the sport has more than just a regional appeal.

Once the International Federation of Strength Athletes adopts IOC prohibitions on steroid use, it seems likely that the sport of strongman will have no upward limit. Strength sports advocates everywhere look forward to that day.

CHRONOLOGY

11th Century	The Scottish Games evolve from a series of strength contests held in Scotland.
1973	David Webster registers the concept of World Heavy Events Championships with British authorities.
1974	The International Olympic Committee bans steroid use.
1976	Russian weight lifter Vasily Alexeyev stuns the world with a record-setting 562-pound lift at the Montreal Olympics.
1977	Universal Studios organizes a televised contest to decide the World's Strongest Man; Olympic weight lifter Bruce Wilhelm wins the inaugural competition.
1980	Bill Kazmaier wins the first of his three WSM titles.
1983	After winning three titles in a row, Kazmaier is dropped from the WSM competition roster.
1984	Jon Pall Sigmarsson of Iceland wins the first of four WSM titles; Sigmarsson wins again in 1986, 1988, and 1990.
1987	World's Strongest Man producers fail to stage a competition.
1991	Another Icelander, Magnus Ver Magnusson, wins the first of four WSM titles; Ver Magnusson wins again in 1994, 1995, and 1996.
1995	David Webster, Douglas Edmunds, and representatives of the athletes form a sport governing body called the International Federation of Strength Athletes.
1997	An exciting new strongman star, Juoko Ahola, wins his first WSM title.
1998	The World's Strongest Man contest is held in Morocco, where a Swedish contender, Magnus Samuelsson, beats Ahola for the title.
1999	Juoko Ahola wins his second WSM title, beating the field in a competition held on the island of Malta; with teammate Janne Virtanen, Ahola wins the World Team Championships in Panyu, China.

MAJOR RECORDS

WORLD'S STRONGEST MAN WINNERS

Year	Name	Contest Location	Country of Winner
1977	Bruce Wilhelm	United States	USA
1978	Bruce Wilhelm	United States	USA
1979	Don Reinhoudt	United States	USA
1980	Bill Kazmaier	United States	USA
1981	Bill Kazmaier	United States	USA
1982	Bill Kazmaier	United States	USA
1983	Geoff Capes	New Zealand	UK
1984	Jon Pall Sigmarsson	Sweden	Iceland
1985	Geoff Capes	Portugal	UK
1986	Jon Pall Sigmarsson	France	Iceland
1987*	Jon Pall Sigmarsson	Scotland	Iceland
1988	Jon Pall Sigmarsson	Hungary	Iceland
1989	Jamie Reeves	Spain	UK
1990	Jon Pall Sigmarsson	Finland	Iceland
1991	Magnus Ver Magnusson	Canary Islands	Iceland
1992	Ted Van Der Parre	Iceland	Netherlands
1993	Gary Taylor	France	UK
1994	Magnus Ver Magnusson	South Africa	Iceland
1995	Magnus Ver Magnusson	Bahamas	Iceland
1996	Magnus Ver Magnusson	Mauritius	Iceland
1997	Juoko Ahola	United States	Finland
1998	Magnus Samuelsson	Morocco	Sweden
1999	Juoko Ahola	Malta	Finland

* **NOTE:** Jon Pall Sigmarsson was the 1987 winner of the Pure Strength competition held at Huntley Castle in Scotland. This is included as no official World's Strongest Man contest was held that year.

WORLD'S STRONGEST MAN RECORDS

THE DEAD LIFT

Competitor	Weight	Where Set	Year
Tom Magee	1177 lbs	New Zealand	1983
Jon Pall Sigmarsson	1133 lbs	New Zealand	1983
Bill Kazmaier	1055 lbs	United States	1982
Ernie Hackett	1055 lbs	United States	1982
Gerrit Badenhorst	968 lbs	South Africa	1994
Juoko Ahola	957 lbs	United States	1997
Don Reinhoudt	950 lbs	United States	1979
Magnus Ver Magnusson	946 lbs	South Africa	1994

THE SQUAT

Competitor	Weight	Where Set	Year
Don Reinhoudt	1000 lbs	United States	1979
Bill Kazmaier	969 lbs	United States	1981
Magnus Ver Magnusson	964 lbs	Bahamas	1995
Ernie Hackett	955 lbs	United States	1982
Tom Magee	955 lbs	United States	1982
Mark Philippi	955 lbs	United States	1997
Dave Waddington	955 lbs	United States	1982
Gerrit Badenhorst	898 lbs	Bahamas	1995
Gary Taylor	898 lbs	Bahamas	1995

THE LOG LIFT

Competitor	Weight	Where Set	Year
Jamie Reeves	374 lbs	Spain	1989
Bill Kazmaier	363 lbs	Spain	1989
Jon Pall Sigmarsson*	360 lbs	Scotland	1987
Raimunds Bergmanis	353 lbs	United States	1997
Gary Taylor	352 lbs	South Africa	1994
Lars Hedlund	346 lbs	United States	1980
Ernie Hackett	345 lbs	United States	1982

* **NOTE:** The 1987 record set by Jon Pall Sigmarsson is from the Pure Strength competition. This is included as no official World's Strongest Man contest was held that year.

MAJOR RECORDS (CONTINUED)

THE BARREL LIFT

Competitor	Weight	Where Set	Year
Don Reinhoudt	300 lbs	United States	1979
Lars Hedlund	290 lbs	United States	1979
Magnus Ver Magnusson	286 lbs	Canary Islands	1991
O. D. Wilson	275 lbs	Canary Islands	1991

THE ROCK LIFT

Competitor	Weight	Where Set	Year
Gerrit Badenhorst	297 lbs	South Africa	1994
Magnus Ver Magnusson	286 lbs	South Africa	1994
Anton Boucher	286 lbs	South Africa	1994
John Gamble	277 lbs	New Zealand	1983
Jon Pall Sigmarsson	275 lbs	Sweden	1984
Laszlo Fekete	275 lbs	Finland	1990

FURTHER READING

Brzycki, Matt, ed. *Maximize Your Training: Insights from Top Strength and Fitness Professionals.* Lincolnwood, Illinois: Masters Press, 1999.

—————. *Youth Strength and Conditioning.* Lincolnwood, Illinois: Masters Press, 1996.

Clarke, Jimmy. *Beginning Strength Training.* Minneapolis, Minnesota: Lerner Publications, 1998.

Hughes, Mary. *The Composite Guide to Bodybuilding.* Philadelphia: Chelsea House Publishers, 2000.

Lund, Bill. *Weightlifting.* Minnetonka, Minnesota: Capstone Press, 1996.

Monroe, Judy. *Steroid Drug Dangers.* Berkeley Heights, New Jersey: Enslow Publishers, 1999.

Peck, Rodney G. *Drugs and Sports.* Bethany, Missouri: Rosen Publishing Group, 1998.

Webster, David. *Sons of Samson.* Nevada City, California: Ironmind Enterprises, Inc., 1997.

INDEX

PICTURE CREDITS Associated Press/WWP: pp. 22, 24, 30, 43; Corbis-Bettmann: p. 14; Library of Congress: pp. 18, 21; Mavrocat Productions/The Strongest Man Alive Contest: pp. 2, 6, 9, 12, 26, 32, 36, 40, 47, 50, 53, 55; Miriam Romais/Photography on the Move: p. 29; Worcester Telegram and Gazette: pp. 38, 58.

MIKE BONNER has written about sports and sports memorabilia for *Sports Collectors Digest, Old Oregon, Beckett Vintage Sports, Sports Cards Gazette, Treasure Chest, Oregon Sports News,* and *Sports Map* magazine. From 1992 to 1993, Bonner wrote a column about the football card hobby for *Tuff Stuff* magazine. In 1993, he solved the mystery of the player on the 1890s Mayo "Anonymous" football card, a hobby landmark. Bonner is also the author of two books on sports trading cards, *Collecting Football Cards,* and *Collecting Basketball Cards.*